This book is to be returned on or before
the last date stamped below. mass.

LIBREX

12560

Heart of England School

778.92

Class ~~720~~

12560

Acc. ~~22273~~

D1807843

FASHION PHOTOGRAPHER

Miriam Moss

FASHION WORLD

FASHION DESIGNER

FASHION MODEL

FASHION PHOTOGRAPHER

STREET FASHION

First published in 1990 by
Wayland (Publishers) Limited
61 Western Road, Hove,
East Sussex, BN3 1JD.

Cover: Fashion photographer Cindy Palmano.

Editor: Janet De Saulles
Designer: Helen White

British Library Cataloguing in Publication Data
Moss, Miriam
Fashion photographer.
1. Photography. Special subjects:
Fashion models – Manuals
I. Title II. Series
778.92

ISBN 1–85210–986–6

© Copyright 1990 Wayland (Publishers) Limited
Phototypeset by Nicola Taylor, Wayland.
Printed in Italy by G. Canale & C. S.p.A. - Turin
Bound in Belgium by Casterman.

CONTENTS

CHAPTER ONE

FASHION AND PHOTOGRAPHY

'THE WORK of a great fashion photographer is the work of the genuine artist.' Yves Saint Laurent, fashion designer.

Fashion photography is often seen as a glamorous job that is done by unusual and highly talented people who lead fast, intense lives. We imagine fashion photographers in exotic locations surrounded by beautiful people wearing fabulous clothes. The best fashion photographers manage to create images which time after time intrigue and surprise us. This requires artistic talent, a perfect technique, a sensitive understanding of subject matter and the ability to sell an image.

Fashion reveals a person's taste and imagination, and can also be used to indicate a rebellion against society. The images made in fashion studios or on location all over the world influence how we look and dress. The photographer has to be alert to fashion trends. Fashion products have to be photographed ahead of time in order to be on time.

Fashion photographs can be defined as pictures made to show or sell clothing or accessories. Striking images help create and sell the latest 'look' in clothes and beauty products. Fashion photographers aim to portray the ideal image of the men and women of the day. Often they make the product more alluring by skilfully drawing us into a world of make-believe.

Above: The clean blues and whites of these Next Directory *fashion clothes convey an idea of a healthy, easy-going lifestyle.*

Opposite: Punk fashion.

This book takes an inside look at the fascinating art and business of fashion photography. Information about the day-to-day work of the fashion photographer is highlighted with comments and advice from some of the most famous international fashion photographers.

THE PARTNERSHIP

Fashion photography provides a very important insight into society: social change is vividly recorded through fashion photographs, revealing the dress, behaviour and attitudes of society. Fashion photographs also reflect how the arts and the business world influence us. Yves Saint Laurent said: 'The fashion pictures I pored over as a boy captured a moment in time forever, and revealed the style, gestures and finery of a certain period.'

Fashion photography has covered many areas in its short history. When photography did arrive on the scene it formed a natural partnership with fashion, which needed the immediate images that photography could provide. The first fashion shots taken in Paris in the 1850s only recorded clothes designs. They were not taken to sell the clothes. True fashion photographs did not reach the public through magazine sales until the turn of the century. From then on the fashion shots seen in *Vogue* and *Harpers Bazaar*, influenced and enchanted the world of fashion.

The first fashion photographer was, perhaps, Baron De Meyer. He created intimate, moody pictures for fashion magazines by using subtle changes in light.

Above: Patrick Lichfield took this picture of Sir Cecil Beaton.

Opposite: American photographer Lee Miller first shot fashion in the late 1920s. During the war period her work went almost exclusively to Vogue.

David Bailey, the photographer 'hero' of the sixties, at work in his studio in London.

Fashion photography was influenced by the changing styles in the art world. In the 1930s when Cubism was making its mark, along with the Spanish artist, Picasso, Edward Streichen introduced a clean, geometric modern style to fashion photography. Cecil Beaton, the famous British photographer, described his work as at the 'opposite end of the photographic pole' to Edward Streichen's. Beaton's fashion shots were fantastic concoctions. He often used strong shadows to create a surrealistic effect. The influence of Art Deco, Surrealism and Hollywood are strong in the fashion photography of the 1930s and 1940s.

The centre of fashion photography moved to New York in the 1950s. There the creative giants, Richard Avedon and Irving Penn, were to be found. Their originality dominated the era. Richard Avedon was famous for the natural quality of his shots. He started working for *Harpers Bazaar* when he was only twenty-one using models whom he called 'real' women unlike the goddess-like women who had modelled before. Irving Penn believed that: 'A beautiful print is a thing in itself, not just a halfway house on the way to the page.' He had a broad knowledge of photography and painting, and said he liked to think of himself as a modern fashion photographer whose work came directly 'from painters of fashion back through the centuries'.

With the free-thinking of the 1960s came the photographer 'hero'. David Bailey fitted this description perfectly. He was part of the rebellious youth culture found in London and he called his fashion photography 'styleless'. It is interesting that during the sixties fashion designers complained that their clothes were just 'props for far-out fashion photography'!

In the 1970s Sarah Moon's fashion photography represented a back-to-nature influence. Guy Bourdin and Helmut Newton, on the other hand, who were working for the French *Vogue,* portrayed fashion in terms of violence and shock. Much of their work reflects the horrific and sensual images in films and the arts, as well as setting the scene for the 1980s with shots which include excessive glamour and wealth. Following on from the harsh, materialistic, self-centred 1980s, the fashion photography of the 1990s reflects a more caring, natural 'green' influence.

CHAPTER TWO

STARTING UP

'I'D GO out with a 35 mm camera and just take photos all over the place, and then I'd print them really badly.' This was how Nick Knight, whose work has appeared in some of the top fashion magazines of the world, started up.

One way to start out in photography is to take one of the many degree and diploma courses available at colleges or polytechnics. You can choose to do a photography course, either full time at college, or as an evening course. Some people join a camera club. Whichever you choose, it is important to make use of the facilities to practise your printing techniques, as using professional laboratories is too expensive for experimentation. Photography is a relatively easy subject to become good at, and a course gives students time to experiment and decide whether they think they can earn a living taking photographs every day.

A college course, however, is not essential and nothing beats getting experience through actually working. As Nick says: 'College taught me to think about what I was doing, but the learning process goes on throughout your life. I don't think you can learn more than when you're actually working.' Many hopeful photographers assist an already well-established photographer.

This method of starting up is traditionally regarded as a sound way into photography. Certainly it is one way to make valuable contacts of your own. The assistant benefits from being totally immersed in the business while learning the ropes. Leland Bobbé, a top fashion photographer who has an established studio in

Australian photographer Polly Borland proves that the equipment used for a shoot can be simple.

New York, says: 'It really is the best way to learn about the business. I learned about getting a portfolio together and taking it around to clients, about how to get jobs and how to deal with art directors, clients and modelling agencies.' To become an assistant you need to seek out photographers whose work you like, and keep on calling them with a view to them seeing your portfolio. Some people assist on a freelance basis. This pays better money but work is not guaranteed.

So what exactly does an assistant's job involve? Leland Bobbé explains: 'Basically it involves doing all the manual and preparatory work on a shoot....making sure there is enough film, that the cameras are loaded, the lights are set up, the equipment is packed and unpacked. I also did all the black and white printing.' Some photographers generously encourage their assistants to test with models, allowing them to use equipment and studios in any free time. This is the best kind of practice available. A good period of assisting builds up confidence and speeds up the process of starting on your own.

There are drawbacks to assisting. The assistant has to get on with the boss who may or may not be interested in teaching the assistant. There are endless stories of assistants being taken for granted, living on a pittance and working unacceptably unsociable hours. Certainly no one becomes an assistant for the money, which is generally regarded as poor. Another pitfall is the danger of the photographer's style influencing the assistant's work. Breaking away from a photographer can also present problems.

Many top photographers have strong reservations about the usefulness of assisting.

Above: This fashion show shot displays the impact that colour makes.

Opposite: The photographer's use of silhouette creates an engaging and sophisticated image.

Nick Knight explains: 'I assisted one of the best British photographers, Brian Griffin. It didn't teach me anything except how he dealt with his problems, and yours are always going to be different.' He continues: 'There are photographers I'd like to assist now, like Paolo Roversi, Bruce Weber, Avedon and Penn. I'd like to see how they do things. But it's just curiosity.'

Many of the famous fashion photographers came to their work through other areas of the fashion industry. Deborah Turbeville, the famous American fashion photographer, started as a fashion editor and then took up photography. Others such as the Italian Tiziano Magni, one of the world's top fashion photographers who originally trained as an architect, are drawn in because their amateur shots catch the eye of an art director.

THE PORTFOLIO

If you want to make a career of fashion photography one important aim has to be to build up a portfolio showing a variety of pictures that you feel represent your talents. Test photography is one way of doing this. In test photography each member of the team involved tests his or her skills. No one receives any payment. The model, stylist and photographer get their own print or transparency from the shoot. If good enough, these go into their portfolios. When a photographer starts out most of the shots will be test shots.

Presenting the work properly is very important. Your portfolio needs to convince people that you can handle an assignment, and

Above: This print has been tinted for special effect.

Opposite: Photographer Sara Leigh Lewis captures a variety of poses.

so a professional approach is vital. You need to include a variety of fashion styles, showing hard and soft lighting for hard or soft fashion. It is a good idea to include some technically difficult shots and a variety of shots from close-up to full figure.

It is worth spending time and money to get top quality prints made and to mount each print on a piece of card. For a sophisticated presentation and to protect the print surface it is a good idea to have individual prints and tear sheets (sheets taken from magazines) laminated by the processing laboratories.

SELLING YOURSELF

When you feel confident about your portfolio, take it round to try and sell your skills to prospective clients. This is the hard slog side of the business when you will need a great deal of faith in your ability, as well as determination and stamina. The lucky break often occurs because you just happen to be in the right place at the right time, and with the right pictures in your portfolio.

If you already have any contact numbers of friends in the business, use them. Build up valuable new contacts by visiting people in the industry with your portfolio. You do not have to limit yourself to editors of top fashion magazines. Go to see trade magazines, independent record labels and designers.

It is important not to be put off if you do not receive a positive response. If your work is radically different, it may take time to be accepted because few art directors, editors and record company executives are very

adventurous at first. But always leave a card with your telephone number on it because occasionally something has to be done at short notice. Many photographers who are just starting out invest in an answerphone so that they are always available.

Professional fashion photographers turn up on time for assignments and spend some time building up a relationship with the people they will be working with. It is important for them to get on well with the team if they want to be offered more work. A professional photographer will find out exactly what the photograph is being used for. For example, a photograph for an album cover may also be reproduced in advertisements, press shots or on T-shirts – all of these uses will influence the content of the final image.

Above: Focusing in on a model – an important fashion shot might be the work of a split second.

Above: A professional photographer carries spare cameras, film, and a variety of lenses and flashes.

Top model Iman Abudulmajid works in Britain and in many other parts of the world. Here she is seen using her own camera.

While this model is photographed, the assistant controls the light falling on the camera lens.

THE EQUIPMENT

Today's cameras are so advanced that a beginner can move relatively quickly to the stage of producing prints which look like magazine images. This user-friendliness makes photography a very popular activity.

The choice of camera for professional fashion photographers is enormous and is a matter of taste and preference. Many swear by large format cameras which have well-defined negatives. These negatives do not lose definition when the images are blown up. There are also medium format cameras and small format cameras (35 mm cameras) which are more easily manageable. The basic starting equipment is a camera and a roll of film. Later, as you build up your equipment, you can add special filters, other lenses and a tripod. When you are ready to start experimenting with printing your shots you could set up your own dark room in a small cupboard. A good DIY photography book will explain how.

Photographic studios can be as huge as aircraft hangars or as small as the tiny canvas tent-like studio Irving Penn made to carry around with him on photographic expeditions. Large or small, the studio is there to give the photographer more control over the finished picture. In the studio the photographer can choose the background and lighting, as well as protecting the subject from the elements such as wind, rain or excessive sunlight.

One important decision when setting up a studio is whether to use tungsten lights or electronic flash. Tungsten lights are cheaper to buy but use up more electricity. An electronic flash freezes all action in the picture but a polaroid test is necessary to see whether the lighting and exposure are correct. When using electronic flash, lighting effects have to be controlled by using umbrellas, diffusers and reflective sheets. There are a multitude of lighting aids which can be used, such as large sheets of expanded polystyrene, foil-covered card and diffusers made of acrylic or tracing paper stretched on a frame.

CHAPTER THREE

THE SHOOT

'EVERY TIME you take a photograph you should take risks.' Nick Knight.

In the early days of fashion photography the shoot simply involved the model and the photographer. Nowadays the shoot is a highly specialized, complicated process. The final image is no longer the work of one imagination, but of a skilled team all making a unique creative effort. Listening to the contributions and judgement of the other members of the team and having a healthy respect for their areas of expertise is vital. A team might include designers, editors, models, hairdressers, make-up artists, art directors, stylists and, of course, the photographer. Each member shares a common aim, which is to create the most effective and up-to-date image possible.

Photographers are only as good as the team around them, so being able to work well with others is important to the fashion photographer's success. Many photographers prefer to work with a tried and tested team. This makes for a really professional atmosphere. Other photographers believe that once the right combination of people has been brought together, an occasional change keeps everyone on their toes.

It is important for the right location to be chosen for the shoot. Fashion photographer, John Stoddart, prefers to use authentic locations rather than studios. He uses an old Rolleiflex camera and maintains that: 'The atmosphere of

Photographer Norman Parkinson, famous for his fashion shots, working on location surrounded by his equipment.

*A fashion shoot can involve a great
deal of discussion.*

real places and the nature of the camera are what gives the pictures their character.' Other photographers prefer the controlled atmosphere of the studio. Some use their own studios or rent larger ones for special assignments.

Once at the location the team starts work. The stylist co-ordinates the clothes, jewellery, props and accessories used in the photographs. Most stylists have no formal qualifications but move into styling via other careers in fashion. A good stylist loves being immersed in fashion. The job means scouring the shops for that vital yellow and black triangular button and collecting last-minute creations from designers, as well as returning them in perfect condition. Simon Foxton, a top stylist, explains: 'There is a lot of leg work involved in styling; you have to know exactly what each shop is selling and what each designer is doing.' Stylists need an excellent sense of colour and an eye for detail, as well as stamina and the ability to work diplomatically with others.

The other members of the team are the make-up and hair artists. In common with models and photographers, make-up artists' agents show potential employers examples of work, such as tear sheets which have been compiled into a portfolio. The work of the beauty artist is not complete even when the model is under the actual lighting and shooting conditions. He or she must work throughout the session making sure that the model's hair and make-up stays in perfect condition.

After the make-up and hair artists have prepared the model, perhaps in consultation with the fashion editor of the magazine or the public relations (PR) person from the advertising company, then the photographer can move in. The photographer's aim is to get the model to co-operate and feel at ease. The saying goes that a nervous sitter will firstly be pre-occupied by being nervous, then the

*Every detail is important: here,
make-up is being retouched.*

A trampoline was used to create a certain look for these models.

nervousness is replaced by boredom, then by pain, and after that the nerves disappear! Some fashion photographers wait and try to capture special moments. Others confront the situation by trying to create and push for things to happen.

The photographer's relationship with the model is perhaps the most significant in making sure the picture is a success. The stereotype image is of a male photographer who manipulates the female model. Alexander Liberman, Art Director of *Vogue* says that the successful female model in the 1940s used to be the one who provoked the photographer, 'through her movement, her expression, her attitude – to fall in love momentarily'. The story today is different.

The emergence today of a great number of women fashion photographers has helped to break the stereotypical relationship between the photographer and model. Sarah Moon is a French model turned photographer who has a special relationship with her models. She says: 'I always work with the same models, which creates a kind of friendship.' Deborah Turbeville goes even further: 'I like to use real, natural people. If it were possible, I would much rather find my subjects on the streets than from an agency.'

The techniques of fashion photographers are as individual as their images. Any real professional, however, takes time to get the exact lighting and positioning of the subject. The creative use of light is vital to the success of the image. Sophisticated modern equipment, such as exposure meters and a vast range of lighting accessories, gives today's photographer much more control over light than in the past. The photographer studies the outline of the model and the positive spaces within a frame. All of these are important to the final success of the

Fashion photographers jostling for position at a fashion show.

Some photographers develop their pictures in their own dark rooms.

picture. The photographer usually shoots a series of test polaroids before exposing any film so that he or she can see how the light falls and how the model, the clothes and the background look. This gives the photographer the opportunity to make any alterations that might be necessary.

Getting the right shot is the aim and this may involve using any number of rolls of film during the shoot. The rolls are then sent off by messenger to the laboratory to be processed. Some photographers develop their own work and spend a great deal of their time staring into their developing tray, reworking an idea. After the fashion shots have been developed, the photographer spreads out the contact sheets on a table, or the slides on a light table, to edit them. The photographer chooses one or two frames which may need to be cropped or enlarged and usually discards the rest. The finished shots are then sent off to the client.

This shot by David Trainer cleverly avoids the sugar and spice look of some children's fashions.

CHAPTER FOUR

THE BUSINESS

'A PHOTOGRAPHER has to be not only a technician and an artist, but also a business person. The photographer has to know how to charge for a job and how to bill for expenses.'
Top fashion photographer Leland Bobbé.

The photographer and the model work together to reflect the elegance of Chanel designs and perfumes.

The fashion photography business is divided into three areas: editorial, advertising and catalogue work, and each has its own special requirements.

Editorial work consists of the fashion shots that accompany the articles and columns of text in magazines and newspapers. This kind of work forms an international sounding board for the talents of fashion photographers. Advertising art directors use magazines as a source book from which to select new photographers. The fees for editorial work are not as high as those for advertising but photographers are credited for their work – their names appear alongside their photographs – and they are less restricted artistically.

A second area of fashion photography is advertising work. Its purpose is to sell a product. It pays well, but when a photographer takes on an advertising job the idea is usually very well established and has been thoroughly planned to fit in with copy and layouts. The amount of input by the photographer is therefore bound to be less than with editorial work. Magazine fashion editors, creative directors, art directors and advertising executives are the people who ultimately have control over the final image. They are the people who decide which photographer to hire.

Make-up and hair artist, Louise Constad, has worked with photographers such as Norman Parkinson and Lord Snowdon, and with pop stars such as Terence Trent D'Arby and Mick Jagger. Her work has appeared in many of the top international fashion magazines. She explains: 'Editorial work is your showcase. Advertising gets you money, but editorial gets you the advertising.' With the enormous amount of photographic material now demanded by the advertising business there is an immense opportunity for work and money. Many photographers support their creative non-fashion work through this kind of outlet. 'Knowing the requirements of the more mundane jobs and seeing them through with style and professionalism are essential to a photographer's livelihood,' says Robert Farber, a top American fashion photographer.

The third area the fashion photographer might be employed in is catalogue work. There are a great many fashion catalogues available and people will order the goods simply by seeing how they look in the photographs. It is, therefore, essential that the photographer makes each item as alluring as possible.

Whatever field the photographer is working in, it is vital to know the different rates of payment. The photographer must be familiar with the rates for newspapers and national magazines, must know the day rates and the page rates for a shoot, and know how much to charge for a black and white or colour advertisement. Nick Knight remembers his first commission: 'When it came to getting paid for it they said how much do you want? And I hadn't got a clue. I had to go and ask a tutor at college!' Nick

A feeling of vivacity and movement has been created in this shot.

agrees that it would have been very easy to ask for too little, especially at the start of his career, but it is bad practice to undercut others. One way of telling how much to charge is that if too much is asked for you will be told immediately, if too little is asked, no one will say anything.

As a photographer's reputation grows, people expect him or her to charge more. Additionally, he or she will need to cover rising overheads. Photography is an expensive business demanding large financial outlays. Expenses include the equipment, the film, the cameras and lenses, the lighting, the expense of creating a portfolio and of advertising, the rental of studios, staff wages and developing costs. There are also other costs such as the insurance covering equipment and people involved on the shoot, travelling expenses, and the cost of the couriers who ferry film and transparencies to and from the laboratories.

Above: These cool cotton Next clothes contrast with the summer heat.

Below: USA photographer, Herb Ritts.

This picture of a men's fashion show details the first model. The line of models behind gives a feeling of continuity.

Fashion photographers also need to spend money on advertising their talents, as this is important to the continuity of the business. American fashion photographers, for example, might take out a page advertisement showing a number of their best pictures in publications like *The Art Director's Index*, *American Showcase* or *The Creative Black Book*.

The business of expenses and payment sorted out, the photographer must set about making arrangements for the shoots. This involves booking models, hair stylists, make-up artists, assistants, and, finally, co-ordinating the whole team. As a business person the fashion photographer often has to be the agent too, making contacts and negotiating with clients. These contacts need to be maintained and promoted by showing work and getting editorial exposure. Specific copyright agreements need to be made with each employer, be it magazine or record company. A friendly agreement written on paper immediately establishes whether the photograph is the photographer's or the property of the people who commissioned the photographer. A photographer will always try to keep any negatives or originals, where at all possible.

In a large fashion photographer's business there may be a back-up team in the form of an assistant, secretary, studio manager and even an agent, but the photographer still has to know every detail of the business. A good agent negotiates the clients' contracts, allowing the photographer to concentrate on the assignments themselves. Methodical book keeping and a good accountant can make all the difference in keeping the photographer's head above water and the tax person at bay.

Getting children to pose on a long fashion shoot requires special skills and expertize.

Another way that fashion photographers make money is through using picture agencies. This is where pictures can be sold over and over again for advertising, magazines, books and posters. The picture agencies organize thousands of photographs to make them easily accessible. Larry Fried, executive vice-president of The Image Bank in New York, one of the largest picture agencies in the world, explains: 'A lot of photographers don't realise what they are sitting on. They have to be reminded that they are in business, that what they have in their hands is merchandise.' Picture agencies make both old and recent photographs work by selling them, drawing in more money for the photographer.

CHAPTER FIVE

THE HOT SHOTS

'YOU MUST move with the evolution of fashion, go with it or before it, but don't let yourself be left behind.' Patrick Demarchelier.

Fashion photography will always operate on the edge between art and the business world, offering a frame through which we see an idealized version of our everyday lives. But fashion is very short-lived and it is not easy keeping in step with it. A fashion photographer's style might be right for this season, but may be totally inappropriate for the next. Nick Knight makes the point: 'To say I'm a fashion photographer and I'm going to produce brilliant fashion photographs until I stop when I'm 80 is unrealistic.' He advises those who have set their sights on being a fashion photographer 'to get it out of their minds, because you can't be a fashion photographer. You have to become a photographer first.'

Top photographer, Lucille Khornak, explains that it is important to be very aware of the darker side of fashion photography: 'This business involves long hours, continual rejection, intense pressure, tight deadlines and explosive temperaments.' Getting established is not easy and it requires patience, a great deal of faith in your own ability and determination. Fashion photographer John Stoddart says his fight to become established was 'not exactly overnight success, but more like steady progress'. And Nick Knight says: 'I can't look at my work in terms of money, jobs or favours, what I'm trying to do with my work is push my life through it.'

The work of British photographer Bruce Weber is featured in the world's top fashion magazines.

Above: Contemporary photographers such as Polly Borland create new and unusual images.

Opposite: Dramatic use of lighting helps the photographer to create sensational fashion shots.

What are some of the drawbacks that the famous fashion photographers encounter? Albert Watson, a Scotsman and one of the most successful fashion photographers working in the USA, has done three advertising campaigns for Chanel. He says: 'My problem is being a workaholic, which is not healthy.' He says he manages to balance his workload by shooting advertising work for American clients while focusing his editorial efforts on European magazines, which, he believes allow photographers greater creativity.

How do the top photographers work? Patrick Demarchelier says he is surprised to find that despite having been a top fashion photographer for twenty-five years he is 'still learning all the time about lighting, about style, and how to talk to people.' He continues: 'Some people work better with bad vibes around them, but I don't think you should be suffering and sweating when you make an image.' His method is not to be concerned about every roll of film and picture he takes: 'I use lots of film, because I am concerned about finding the right moment.'

Many of the top photographers agree that success depends on developing a unique personal style. A photographer's style is what makes his or her pictures special and individual. John Stoddart says: 'I don't think that my work is necessarily revolutionary, but it is mine and I think it has something individual to say.' Lucille Khornak believes that success as a fashion photographer is to do with being alert to trends: 'preferably not after they happen, but just before. You need to anticipate the next significant step in fashion. For a good fashion photographer,' she says, 'these skills are second nature.'

GLOSSARY

Art Deco   A style of interior decoration and architecture at its height in the 1930s and characterized by geometric shapes.

Contact print   A photographic print made by exposing the printed paper through a negative placed directly on to it.

Contact sheet   A sheet of contact prints.

Copy   Material that is going to be reproduced in print.

Cropped   Made smaller.

Cubism   A school of art started in 1907 by the artists Picasso and Braque.

Dark room   Room where photographic film is processed and developed.

Laminated   Sealed inside plastic.

Layouts   The arrangement of text, photographs or artwork for printing.

Negative   A piece of photographic film that has been exposed and developed.

Overheads   Business expenses.

Polaroid   The print that a polaroid camera produces in seconds by processing and developing the picture inside the camera.

Prints   The black and white or colour images produced from negatives.

Surrealism   A movement in art and literature in the 1920s characterized by placing strange and unusual images together to produce a dream-like quality.

Tear sheets   Fashion features which have been cut out of magazines and kept for future reference.

Transparencies   Also called slides. A positive photograph on a transparent base.

Tungsten   A hard greyish-white element used in lamp filaments.

FURTHER READING

Careers in Fashion by Carole Chester (Kogan Page, 1989).

Fashion Photography: A Professional Approach by Lucille Khornak (Amphoto, an imprint of Watson-Guptill Publications, 1989).

Patrick Demarchelier: Fashion Photography (Little and Brown, 1989).

Professional Fashion Photography by Robert Farber (American Photographic Book Publishing, Amphoto, an imprint of Watson-Guptill Publications, 1981).

The Fashion Photographer by Robert Farber (American Photographic Book Publishing, Amphoto, an imprint of Watson-Guptill Publications, 1981).

For examples of the work of fashion photographers look in any of the international glossy fashion magazines such as British, Italian, French, German and US *Vogue*; French, Italian, British and US *Harpers Bazaar*, *Elle* and *Cosmopolitan*. Those found specifically in the USA: *Glamour*, *Mademoiselle* and *Gentleman's Quarterly*.

ACKNOWLEDGEMENTS

All Action (Duncan Raban) 14 (bottom), 15, Robin Kennedy 20 (left); Polly Borland 9, 28; Camera Press (Patrick Lichfield) 7, (Clive Arrowsmith) 23; Sara Leigh Lewis 13; Lee Miller (David E Sherman) 6; Next Directory 4, 24 (top); Rex Features 5, 8, 10 (Sylvan Mason) 17, (Robert) 22, (Young) 24 (bottom), (Bartheleny) 25, (Brooker) 26, (Sichov) 27; Frank Spooner (Edelhajt Winczewski) 14 (top), (Eric Brissaud) 16, Piquemal Figaro 18 (top): Topham 11, 18, (bottom), 19, 20 (top), 29; David Trainer 12, 21.

The author and Publisher would like to thank *Next Directory* for all their help.

INDEX

Numbers that appear in **bold** refer to captions.